MW01025631

Empty Buckets

⧖

Ms. Joanne Gordon:

I thank you for your support in my efforts. Please know that my contributions are genuine in this book. I appreciate your support!

Cameron Lewis

C. L. Lewis

Copyright © 2010 by C. L. Lewis.

ISBN: Softcover   978-1-4535-1289-0

All rights reserved. No part of this book may be reproduced or transmitted in any form
or by any means, electronic or mechanical, including photocopying, recording, or by
any information storage and retrieval system, without permission in writing from the
copyright owner.

This book was printed in the United States of America.

To order additional copies of this book, contact:
Xlibris Corporation
1-888-795-4274
www.Xlibris.com
Orders@Xlibris.com
77668

DEDICATION:

This poetry collection is dedicated to the many sources of inspiration in my life:

- *God, The Highest Power*

- *My Friends & Family*

- *The Power of Love*

- *Those I've Misunderstood and/or Who have Misunderstood Me*

- *Those who Struggle in Life but Persevere*

Special thanks to T. Jordan, B. Miller, J. Wilkinson, R. Dominico, & C. Fouch

Table of Buckets

What is Empty Buckets About?

"Empty Buckets" represents the story of my life. For several years now, I have referred to the positive situations in my life as 'Buckets'—which stems from my love of basketball (my circle of family, friends, and co-workers can identify here). But in my case, 'buckets' also symbolize all positive forms of life: from the literal definition of scoring when on the basketball court, to doing well in other aspects of daily life. Over time, the term 'buckets' in my life came to specifically define the "success" of having many romantic interests from women. The purpose of this collection is to explore this and the many other forms of 'buckets' that have made my life what it is today.

The focus of this book is on my life as an Empty Bucket, a lonely place with no substance. The romantic 'buckets' I refer to also have no substance because the true meaning of who I am is still missing and trying to be discovered. Currently I feel as though I am misunderstood. Through a series of my poetry and live-letters, I will try to explain who I really am, and this is where I will identify the potential for more meaningful 'buckets' in my life. It is my hope that by releasing this piece of me I can actively address the issues within my past and thus move forward to becoming a better man in my future.

C. L. Lewis

<u>Empty Buckets</u>

Still doing childish things but I need to be past that
Others need motivation, "Be something to look at,"
I say to myself while looking in the mirror
When face-to-face with myself like that it can't get any clearer

But my reflection will not show my vision or plan
The goal is to function like the Allstate man
Where I'm helping the world with the strength of BIG HANDS
Performing so well people rest assure that I can
For now this dream rests in back of my eyes
You wouldn't know the truth if I didn't tell you, or until you've
read these lines

Mr. Buckets

Each day is a new day to make history.
I'll be there.
Take a look at what I see . . .

<u>Deep Within</u>

Deep within me is a good man and I know it. Deep within me I can achieve success, but how do I show it?

To grow up I've depended on a much slower process because at an early age I never quite received the best demonstration of what it takes to be a man

I believe the success will arrive soon, just as my potential for growth because these 2 things go hand-in-hand

<u>*Just Me*</u>

The story of my life . . .

Alone in a dark room consumed by my thoughts

Prayers of escape from my flaws and fears

Hate, Paranoia and Lust trap my soul and ignite a burning fire within my mind

My hearts is at war as my need for love and comfort encounter my predisposed notions of anger and attack

But somehow I manage to control my conflicting affairs well enough to present to the world what I want them to see

For now I have nothing . . . No trust, No love, No fear

Just myself and the life that hides my would-be tears

Alone

People don't know why I'm a loner.

But I've been left alone so many times that it's the only thing that feels like home.

And therefore now I leave others before they can leave me.

Part of it is for protection and the other part is that it has become a comfort for me.

<u>My Mental Highway</u>

Moving slow in a fast world
My speed is so different
People can't catch me but I can't keep up with them
Is time on my side or is it against me?
It may be that others are running at safe speeds
Or it may be that I am protecting me from me, or protecting me
from sin, protecting me from them—the other people that is

The noise that they're making around me is just a blur in the
background
My thoughts are too many, so there's nothing they can do for me
They laugh outside. Inside I worry, then laugh, then get mad
But then I must hurry
My racing thoughts are too fast for the average
And realistically too fast for me even, but it's what I deal with
because I have it

Full Circle

We have come full circle now, my pops. I'm torn with what I should do. I could be myself and show you love, but this is something my heart does not want to do. On the flipside I could do nothing—just sit back and ignore your existence . . . payback so to speak. But in the end I gain nothing and only prove that it is I who am weak.

We have come full circle now, my pops. I am a man in my own right. Living my life day-by-day and trying to do what's right. But your life has become my life. Your blessings are my blessings; your curse is my curse. Even still, as hard as I fight to be better than you are, I could very well still turn out worse.

Chances are you don't get it. You don't know the damage you have done to my heart. I've learned to try and hide it all; to keep my past and present apart. My future is the promise ahead and I rarely look back. But in those brief moments of reflection I realize that I should give you some credit for where I'm at. Because even in your negligence, you have groomed me. For the good and the bad that I am, and the person I aspire to be.

We have come full circle now, my pops. Years have passed and lessons have been learned. In the time to come may the Lord above mend the bridge that was once burned?

<u>Face 2 Face</u>

The time will come when you'll have to be yourself
When you've tried as hard as you could but come up short
Tried to lay in the background but you stood out too loud
Then you made a big scene so others would notice, but still you
seemed too proud

So where does that leave me now?

To be the only way I can be
The fun-loving, sometimes serious me
The work-of-art I was put on this earth for others to see
As I try to grow and groom myself to a standard I may never reach
I can never escape just who I am so I must live my life for keeps

Who Loves You?

The greatest love I've ever known in the physical form is the love you've given to me. I am your first born. A mistake on earth, but the truth in God's eyes. When He made you He made me. God's love is your love and that is what you've given to me.

How can I find a repayment?

I know there is no tangible gift that can say what you mean to me. But my heart is the answer and key. It has the same love and care that you have placed in my life. My tears are for you—for the pain that we have endured together & the strength you have shown through it all.

And how do I live without you? I do not ever!

I keep you within me forever as my torch. The fuel that has made it possible for me to run this long! I wish that I could achieve the greatness that you deserve so that we can shine together with Glory to God. Maybe one day it will be so—of that I do believe. I pray that we can celebrate those moments together.

Whether on Earth or in Heaven.

A Piece of Me

I have never really been able to get people to appreciate my physical voice. One way or another it never comes across properly. Whether people don't understand me or I just don't speak with enough command and authority. I am unsure to exactly what the reason is. What I do know is that this experience has caused me a great deal of stress and confusion throughout my life; at times even a great deal of grief. But the value in the words I write is that they have the power to stand-alone. They do the thing that I am not able to do. They speak to you (and hopefully you listen and hear them for what they're worth). So when you decide to read know that what I've given is genuine. A piece of me indeed . . .

Buckets of Love

The heart is delicate. The head is hard.
Now to protect myself, I put up my guard.

Degree of Separation

The difference between making love and having sex is the amount of RESPECT that comes along with the action. It can be a matter of future enjoyment or dreaded regret. Depending on whether you receive esteem or neglect.

What separates love from lust is similar to the components of jealousy and TRUST. A fine line that can be crossed on either side-depending on whether you wait or you rush.

Both lust and love could be a kiss or a hug, but will you know the difference when the feeling is sent from above? A look is not the same as a gaze. One is a temporary feeling. The other has the power to leave you in a daze that will last for days.

Night Vision

I saw you in a dream the other night. I was mesmerized by your eyes, just as in real life. Eyes that capture my heart when they make contact with mine.

Although only for a split second, there is a feeling I get each time that is impossible to describe . . . somewhere between love and lust, a combination of nervous and excited. That is me when I see you . . .

How did you make your way into my dream? We have never met or spoken, but if our eyes can communicate then you know exactly how I feel about you. Just a chance to know you would give me satisfaction.

That way I could determine if you are really my dream come true. It's quite possible that I could be yours too. In the meantime if I should fall asleep and come across you in my dream again, I will do my best not to wake up until I can bring you back with me.

<u>*Watching*</u>

I feel your energy every time you say "hi." At that very time I am flooded with feelings. You are so beautiful that you appear flawless. The butterflies in my stomach are making me shy. This tingling sensation has me questioning "why?"

It would make sense for me to approach you and confess my feelings. But when I think I've found the words to say, all that comes out is a "goodbye."

So now I am forced to live in my own self-imposed trap of emotion, and hope that you don't forever pass me by.

P. H. A. T.

Gorgeous face with a wonderful smile.

P. H. A. T.

Smoking hot body. Sexy long legs.

P. H. A. T.

Move those hips. Purse those lips.

That's P. H. A. T.

Smell so good. All the time.

P. H. A. T.

Can be naughty or nice. But always right ☺.

P. H. A. T.

Confident that you're # 1. Won't settle for less. Would rather have none.

That's P. H. A. T.

So when I call you 'FAT' know that you're just that.

Pretty, Hot, And Tempting.

Bless You

Like the woman of my dreams, you cannot possibly be true, but still I continue to imagine. Looking at you draws me in like quick sand . . . as I drown into the unknown I only wish that I could be familiar with you.

Not even these words can describe the interest that I have inside. While I cannot lie and say that it is more than a physical attraction, I can honestly say to you that I am not that type of guy.

Though I like what I see, I will not disrespect you with trivial pursuit. Instead I will admire from afar and wish nothing but the best for you.

<u>*Torro*</u>

You snuck upon me like a thief in the night, with stunning beauty and a body so tight. For some reason I could not get you out of my sight. I wanted to pursue you but didn't feel the time was right. I was wrong.

You captured me as though I were in a trance; with a spicy attitude to accompany a sexy dance. Even more unique because you were willing to take a chance. With that you inspired me and my new year.

You showed your value by the strength of your mind. Living, learning, and fighting all of the time. Continuing to prove yourself to be one of a kind . . .

<u>My Packaged Gift</u>

Your mind tells a story that I'm dying to read

A voice so delicate and soothing it creates music for my ears

Complementing such is an enticing figure which brings a smile

to my face while fueling my racing heart

Your attitude combines sugar and spice-making a recipe for success

Even greater within lies a pure soul

A treasure to be received by only the most fortunate ☺

Phase 1: Warm-up

<u>Waiting</u>

Press your lips upon mine.

Don't run away for I am here to stay.

So if you want to run and hide just know I won't be far behind.

See this is a journey for you and I.

And alone is worse than side by side.

So don't prolong the ride.

The Heart of War

I declare war upon you
As you stand readily behind your fortress, anticipating my attack
You understand the reasoning for my gesture, so you decide to
hold back
Rather than step out from your protection to engage in a battle
with me
You fail to acknowledge my assault and ignore this enemy

But if only you would look out it would be so clear to see
I come in peace; I will bring you no harm
I seek to protect you with the strength of my arm
I will serve as your shelter in the midst of a storm
Even be your clothing when you need to be warmed

There is no need to hide from what I want to share with you
It is only my love and these feelings are true
But continue to take cover if you feel that you must
Because I will climb this fortress if that means gaining your trust

<u>We Connect!</u>

Those eyes are drawing me near . . . telling me that you want me so close to your body that I forget we are 2 and not 1.

But if we were any closer we would be none.

'Cause we are so deep into each other that we sometimes fall into a place where there is nothing at all.

No people, no faces, no bodies, no names . . . Just love, passion, and sexual games.

The place we've fallen to doesn't exist to others, so we think we've disappeared like kids do when they hide under covers.

More than lovers, we enjoy companionship and friendship.

TOGETHER

So this moment we share will never end unless it is beginning again!

<u>That Night</u>

I don't know if our paths were destined to cross.
Through the course of our interaction we established an extraordinary bond.

On this special night I found myself in an unlikely place doing unlikely things. Then once all of the excitement and celebration of my travels concluded, there you were. Although impaired by drinks and joy, I have a clear perception of the moment I crossed the street and made contact with you at the corner.

Both out of our element but still We Connect!
Now I can understand the meaning of being at the right place at the right time.

<u>*Moonlight*</u>

Underneath the moon is where there were 2. The 1st experiences that would eventually lead to an "I love you." Who knew it would start here? It was an uncontrolled chemistry that may have been caused by the moon's glare.

With no stars in the sky but a moon so bright, these 2 friends were having a fight. But not mad—rather understanding each other. In fact, enjoying each other's company; this is how friendship is supposed to be.

So under the moon they stood and talked. Love was in the air though they were unaware. They drew nearer to each other, lost in a deep gaze. You'd be amazed to know it wasn't a movie or TV show. It was the look in their eyes that reflected the moon's glow.

They drew closer without losing sight of each other amidst the dark night. With only the moon's light to show them the way, their lips touched and they embraced in a new way.
This first kiss was something they'll remember 4 life. And they'll forever and always be connected 2 each other by the moonlight . . .

That's All . . .

All I want to do is look in your eyes . . . Beautiful . . . When our eyes meet from afar our temperatures rise.

All I want is to be blessed with your smile . . . Glittering . . . Just to see a grin I'll cross an ocean for miles.

All I want to do is lay on your chest . . . Soothing . . . The way you reassure me when I'm fed up with stress.

All I want to do is caress your legs . . . Enticing . . . so soft and smooth you make every man want to beg.

All I want to do is go for a ride . . . Sweet Love . . . I jus hope you will welcome my love inside.

All I want is to run my fingers through your hair . . . and let you know that no matter what happens in your life I'll be there.

Let me place my arms around the small of your back . . . as I squeeze I get lost in the moment and forget where I'm at.

All I want to do is hold your feet . . . and kiss and rub them to make your hard day complete.

All I ask is that I take your hand . . . so that from this day forth I'm forever your man.

All I need is a piece of your mind . . . because everyone knows that true love is blind. But you have inner beauty and I love it.

All I need is a piece of your heart . . . as you have had mine from the start . . .

~That's all I need!

<u>Cheers!</u>

May I propose a toast? Sometimes people become so special to you, so much a part of your heart that you want them closer.

You want to intertwine your being with theirs—and combine mind, body, and spirit like wrapping vines.

To merge into 1 like grapes that become wine . . . so fine over time.

If that were the case then you would be mine.

Maybe one day you will if it's part of God's plan.

But even if not, I will always be yours as a friend, brother, or potential man.

Life is about sacrifice and I understand that, but my imagination is greedy so in my mind I pretend that—

Circumstances were not the same. Maybe we would build a family together and eventually share my last name.

But instead of living regrets, I'll be thankful for you, the special friend I've been so happy to get. Cheers!

The Blueprint

You are the open book I crave to read. The realest woman I can recall indeed. I appreciate your sincerity. And I have come to realize that within you there is something that I need.

I love that you never hold back unless you are holding my back. Because you definitely care for me and have taken care of me like only a proven love would do. For that I will forever give my heart to you.

You may never know what you mean to me. The standard of what I strive to be. The goal of what I wish to have, when I call someone my other half.

If I cannot have you in my life forever, then I will thank you now for making me see. I owe you so much in this world, but all I can give to you is ME.

<u>*Comfort*</u>

It is so fulfilling when I can run my fingers through your hair. And watch you sleep as I hold you close.

The way the moonlight shines on your pretty face in a room that is otherwise filled with darkness. It's like God has placed the ultimate spotlight upon you in order to show me the true beauty of your presence. You look so calm and at ease with the world.

Meanwhile I am trapped amidst two feelings . . . as on the one hand, my heart races with the thrill and excitement of being so close to perfection. I lose myself in the reality that I share life with you.

At the same time, I can look at you and see both your inner child as well as your current womanhood. You are the constant symbol of warmth and all that I admire.

Looking at you in this state helps me to find relaxation. Your peace becomes my peace. Without you even realizing it, we share the purest intimacy. As you sleep—I live a dream.

Never Ever . . .

Never have I felt more comfortable with someone.

Never have I connected so well. I have never been so excited to see one face or hear one voice.

Never have I smiled and laughed so much. I have never seen a face more beautiful or a woman so attractive.

Never have I been so turned on by intelligence and grace.

Never have I cared so much about someone.

Never have I been so concerned.

Never have I admired someone so. I have never been so attached.

Never have I missed such a presence.

Never been so close to something perfect for me. I have never met someone so special . . .

That is until I met you.

<u>Slow Motion</u>

Pause this moment

Freeze this frame

Hold on tight and savor the same

A time like this might not come back again

Where your senses speak a language you can't quite understand

An explosion of love again and again

When eyes meet they lock together at a rate that no distraction could break

Every kiss has a meaning

Every touch draws a feeling

And hugs are a force-field created by two

That energy is stronger than both me and you

My Real Love

I wish I had the ability to do something that I felt could truly demonstrate how I feel about you. But I can't at the moment and only God knows why. I do have my love for you and I hope this will suffice for now. Because whether you know it or not, whether you feel I show it or not, my love for you is real. Not like those ideal TV shows and movies with those fantasy situations. Real.

Real like love is real. With all of the ups and downs that come with being in a relationship. A love that is worth being in a relationship because it is real. I can say that my feelings for you are genuine and true. Whether I am mad or happy, jealous or indifferent, you can rest assure that I am giving you my all. Not perfect, but a work in progress which is what life is anyway. A journey to improve each day while learning and finding meaning.

I just wish that I could somehow do more to display to you who I am—what I think and how I feel. If I could just do something to make you see—then you would understand and appreciate the Real Love inside of me. You can have my heart to keep if you choose. While it will not speak words directly to you, if you listen to the rhythm and intensity of its beat you will understand that it plays music from my soul. Although you cannot determine the origin of my lyrics, I welcome you to dance to my never-ending song which draws from you as a source of its inspiration.

<u>*Distant Love*</u>

Within my heart you have found a special place. The only thing that separates us now is space. I've heard about those who have let special girls pass by, but with you there is not a second to waste.

I believe that we have a real connection. I love to hear your voice, but I never get to see your face. You have gotten very close to my heart from a distance so far. At times I want to be where you are.

I could see us watching TV for hours—laughing and joking, or wrestling each other like sister and brother. I could even see candles lit with you under covers, and me in front of the radio playing "Distant Lovers."

But for the meantime, I want you to know that I appreciate you. Not for anything more than just being you!

FF's (Friends Forever)

You will always have a special place in my heart, for the way your presence pierced it like an arrow.

You entered my life at a unique point and gave me something that is hard to come by in this world—Friendship.

As you opened your heart to me, I gave you mine in return.

Even though things have changed between us now, when we look back and reflect nothing can erase the beauty of the time we've spent TOGETHER.

Phase 2: Crunch Time

<u>Strength</u>

There once was a young man that everyone perceived to be strong.
He appeared so strong that people often asked,
"Is there nothing that can weaken that man?"

How about the beauty of an angelic face that looks like the
pathway to heaven? With eyes like stars that light the dark sky
and leave him as vulnerable as a meteor floating in outer space.
A smile that even from the furthest distance of view makes his
heart melt. This beauty is so intoxicating that he sometimes fears
that another man stronger than he will come and take her away.
Is that all?

What about the warmth of a kind heart? A heart so kind and
caring that at times the strong man feels like nothing but a
defenseless baby, desperately in need of nurturing from his
mother. While this strong man wants nothing more than to
support and protect his lady, her support for him becomes so
regular that he becomes insecure with himself and doubts his
own usefulness as a man. Is there anything else?

Even more is the brilliance of a mind that offers a unique challenge to his. From time to time the differences in opinion make him uncomfortable, nevertheless he admires the fortitude shown whether in disagreement or harmony. However, the power of her mind is so intense that the strong man becomes skeptical and worried that their differences will one day cause them to separate.

So is there anything that can make this strong man weak? Yes, there are actually a couple of things. Yet not to worry, all of these things have been packaged and given to him as a gift from God rather than as an opposition or enemy.
She is a strong woman. She is you!

Your Love

These hands of mine are not the strongest of hands, but my love for you will allow me to hold you forever . . . with a grip too tight for anything to penetrate our bond.

My feet are flat, tired and aching. My legs are weak and my knees are bad. But when your love calls, I will be there:
To walk you home
To walk you to the door
To walk with you through the park or the sands of the beach
And in the times when you are far away, the thought of being without you will make me run to get closer to your love.

When I look in the mirror, I am not always satisfied with what I see. So I compare myself to others and wish that I could make changes. But when I am with you I realize that my thoughts were foolish. You reassure me of who I am:

The way that you look at me
That flirtatious smile that you give me to excite my day
The way that you say my name
The touch of your hands when we embrace

I realize the intensity of your love for me. You admire me in the most uplifting way . . . the way that only you can. You give me confidence when I need it, and for this I thank you.

I am not the most intelligent man in the world . . . but I can accept that because I have you. Your love makes me a stronger person and I am a better man for being with you. Therefore I am the smartest man in the world. In you, I have found the meaning of life and the answer to all of the world's problems.

IT'S LOVE . . . Your Love to be exact!

<u>*Disappearing Act*</u>

What happened to that girl I used to know?

The one that took my heart and soul

Had me speechless, and thankful to walk beside her

Standing tall proud to be in her presence

Thinking future instead of present or past

Cherishing time because it told the story for each of our moments together

But somewhere along she vanished without a trace

Left me with no answers or no real goodbye

I just wish I knew why?

<u>*My Bad*</u>

It must be me

Must be me that is causing us to disagree

I become upset because I care

I get jealous when I think someone else is there

I try to protect you but push you away

I want to communicate but somehow I sent you astray

I can't understand it

Maybe it would have worked better if I planned it

Or saw my mistakes in time to correct them

Wasn't observant enough to pick up on your signals to me

From your perspective I chose to neglect them

Spud in the Mud

She dropped me like a hot potato and passed me all around

Then cut me into curly fries and put me in a fire to drown

She watched me burn in a pool of grease and fed me off like a piece of meat

Now I'm crushed like a potato chip that's been stepped on by her feet

<u>*And Another One*</u>

She's just another empty bucket

When times get tough she'll come my way, looking for me to save the day

Provide the attention she's been missing

Talk her through problems and be there to listen

But when better days come she'll be sure to go missing

Back to that which brings her comfort

In the process leaving me for dead and to feel so hurt . . .

And that doesn't work, but nevertheless she's in and out of my life

Mostly out-only in when the time is right, for her

So to describe her, 'another empty bucket' is what I say

Because she's here one minute, but the next she's gone astray

The Mind of the Man

Don't make decisions about us without me. That's supposed to be a—we thing. Then once I've done something that doesn't match your plan that somehow makes me become less of a man?

Don't assume I know what you want. For me, we haven't agreed on it unless we've discussed it up front. The next thing I know I have to explain that things are different and you're not what I want . . . But I never said you were in the first place.

Not trying to be rude but I have to be real. We've got to lay it all on the line when we're making a deal. Let's not mistake what we think from what we feel. That's the difference between my mind and yours.

C. L. Lewis

Distance

My heart won't lie to me if I listen
And the feeling I hear now is loud and crystal
Clear to me that we have drifted apart
Like two sides of a broken boat
Travelling toward opposite sides of the world as we float
The sun from the dark or the light from the moon
As time changes these things move away to make room for one
another

A shock to the heart
I believe in the joy of love that's right from the start
But this feels empty
Something is missing
May we both find a new way is what I'll be wishing?

Turn the Page

Turn the page.
The look in your eyes has changed.
That sparkle in your eye is gone.
You don't have to say a word, I know it's over.
There's no tool that can repair the damage I've done to your heart.

Because of that I have no words.
There is nothing I can say to sway your heart or your mind.
Oddly enough these signs tell me that I can never again make you mine.
So my consequence is a lonely life.
No second chance—with you at least.

This chapter is over.
I've lost my time in your life but I cannot cry.
I'd rather hide my feelings inside.
I deserve to suffer in this way while I am still alive.
Close the book. Move on.

C. L. Lewis

Free Time

The time has come to be free from you.
Your time has come to be free from me.
It hurts so much and we'll always know.
But this can be chalked up to destiny.
From the start I felt that it couldn't be.

From the start you felt that it shouldn't be.

So now time has passed and we're thinking we'd be better on our
own—wouldn't we? The time for lies has come and gone.
What's right was right. What's wrong was wrong.
This dance of ours has come and gone so now it's time for another
song.

No Regrets/Farewell

NO REGRETS

I talk to so many older adults that are completely miserable in their lives-wishing that they could go back and fix things in their pasts. I'm seeing that I'm on the path to being the same way at this rate, but I don't want to be. I want to be happy and great. So now I'm going to step out and stop being afraid. Just be me. That means doing things that fit my personality and the awkward but special person that I am. That's what I'll try to do from here on out. No Regrets!

FAREWELL

I've really been feeling a need to see you and be around you in my heart. I didn't want to miss an opportunity at a true soul mate. But I did. I let it slip. I just want you to know—you should have someone in your life that is your everything. If it can't be me, make sure you find it. Because life is too short for anyone to deny their heart or the signs in front of them. I guess the signs say otherwise for us. I take total responsibility for where things are right now. It is my fault through and through. I'm sorry for that. Your life is in a different place now and you have let me go. The logical part of me understands. So despite where my feelings are now I can only respect your decision. I'll step back. The emotional side of me does not see it the same way. But it was my mistake and I'll work through that on my own with the rest of my issues. I want the best for you. Whoever and whatever that is. I will deal with my feelings in my own way-on my own. But still always here for you if necessary . . . please never forget that. My heart is torn, but at the same time I am glad and thankful that the Lord has given me this insight now. I love you.

Always and Forever

C. L. Lewis

<u>*Dusty Road*</u>

Dragging my feet down this dusty road
Can't turn back unless the wind blows
Can't stand to see what I've left behind
So afraid, but walking proud to suppress the thoughts in my mind
My heart is breaking with every step
I hope time will cure the pain I've left

I must move on
I don't want to but I must
So Lord please blow the wind to show a cloud of dust
That way when I look back I can't see what I've left
And she won't see my eyes to know that I've wept

I'm holding my head high but dragging my feet
My heart pounds my chest as each boot hits the street
Turn back—I want to—so bad in my mind
But the hour glass is now empty
I've run out of time

Heartache

There is a stamp on my heart with your name on it. You put a spell on me girl and I just can't call it. I can't understand it. There's something so romantic with how you made me fall deep for you and never planned it. I never saw it coming, but felt it deep down inside that your soul was desperately reaching for mine. Or mine was seeking yours. But either way I know I've never felt a better love than yours. I can't describe the pain I feel, when I think now that you've gone so far away and we never quite sealed the deal. Not talking about sex. I'm talking commitment. The way we were together could've taken it to the finish. I'm talking about kids. I'm talking about the house on the hills with yard, dog, pool, and the picket fence. That was supposed to be, forever you and me. But I couldn't love you right so now it's history.

<u>*Almost Maybe*</u>

If I could have you back I would take you in a heartbeat, with no second thoughts. But I refuse to force my way back into your heart or beg for your love. Should you come back to me it must be on your own, so I'm letting you go to find where you belong.

If I could be the perfect man for you I would—try—my best for the rest of my time. But I can't seem to erase my need to be a predator that seeks new prey every day. I need constant prayer and divine intervention to reach my potential and one day arrive.

If I could make this world be a place for only you and me, it'd be the happiest place you'd want to see. Yet there's no changing what has come of you and me. Our lives are similar but also quite different, which makes the distance between our hearts strangely both close and far.

The odds are clearly stacked against us, but there is hope wherever love exists. There is love from our Father above. So if he sees fit for us to share our love then maybe He will make a true 'US' out of you and me.

<u>Refuse</u>

Can't accept the fact that you're gone. Tell me what I have to do to be with you. I will come where you are. I will bring you back to me. But I know that I need you in my life.

So scared without you. I refuse to lose your love. I'd rather give away any money or cars. All the old love in my life and past emotional scars. They have brought me to this moment of realization.

I can't take not having you in my life. Better yet, I can't shake the feeling of wanting to make you my wife. But what do you say? You refuse . . .

C. L. Lewis

Too late

If you're going to come back, don't wait
I would hate for it to be too late
Don't allow the time to pass and my life to change
Over time my direction will turn-as will my feelings—and from
that point we'll never be the same

Don't wait until it's too late
Don't wait until another man has damaged your heart
I am not the safe bet and I will not be waiting until you notice
regret and then come back saying that I was really the one from
the start. So sad it's too late

If you choose to go different than me best wishes
Live to the fullest because I will do the same
If that means you're married with kids to another then who do
we blame?
Aww man, it is too late
Our time together ran out, but that was just fate

New Love

New love I need you. Take my mind off the old love or whatever I thought she was. She couldn't have been love could she? Because if she was we wouldn't be at odds right now, would we? But anyhow I'm talking to you my new love and only you. I'm excited to return to doing the things that new love can do. Give me that fresh feeling because everything is brand new. And it's only great because you don't really know me, and I don't know you.

But after a while the new look fades and we question this new love because we don't understand each other's ways. Now I'm thinking back to better days. Thinking of how much I've missed old love's ways. Questioning why I ever went away. I thought that new love was the answer but the question remains how could I ever replace my old love if those feelings have stayed?

<u>Broken Promise</u>

I have to apologize with all my heart.

When I saw you yesterday, all I could think of was the fact that it has been two years and I never called. Please believe that it was not my goal to be shady or insincere.

Unfortunately though, I knew that my intentions with you were not right at the time. If I were to offer you anything then, it would have only been a temporary test. A situation that would have only led to my selfish desires causing you to become upset.

So my best reaction was to avoid the situation. I know now that I could have gone about this in a better way. But when I looked at you I could feel your disgust. I could tell that you had nothing to say to me because I had betrayed your trust. The shame for my part in the situation would not allow me to put together any explanation. There is no excuse for my actions. All I can say is that I am sorry and I hope that one day you will be able to forgive me.

Beautiful Ladies!

I'm familiar with your type
Beautiful ladies!
Met so many in my time
Beautiful ladies!
In all shapes and sizes
Married with babies
But I do admire my
Beautiful ladies!
On the outside gorgeous
Hair, skin and size
On the inside caring
But I like the eyes
I like the smile
I like the laugh
I love the soul
I want to hold you
But I play the background
It's best to avoid you
See I'm no good
Cold-hearted in fact
They call me 'Killa' for that reason
Hearts will get cracked
So a warning to all my
Beautiful ladies!
I'm no good
A little too crazy
A lot of a loner
And I'll make you crazy
I'm lusting for all my
Beautiful ladies!

<u>Silly Me</u>

I can't deny that your love is real

But still I chase other would-be types for the thrill

I'm always looking for bigger and better, but maybe I'm still

looking because I've overlooked what you're willing to give me

Where would-be won't, you will and continue to do well

So imagine how much like a fool I now feel???

Endless Love

We've been at this for years now. Through the ups and downs, feelings of love and hate we still seem to have a life together. How? After all these years and all these tears, I've been looking for you to help me overcome my fears. But that's all up to me—because through these years you've been right here with your heart and a love that wants to be sincere.

Sure you've failed at times, and so have I, but in a life built on emotions what makes you smile is bound to make you cry. In my time of denial I have tried to program my emotions by forgetting about you and hating our past. But silly of me to think that I could overcome the power of a love built to last.

Right now we live separate, unsure of each other. One day we will reach our destiny together, 1 way or the other. Whether as friends or lovers, I carry your energy from now until all light is dark and I live no more. For now we'll just soar on our crazy love track.

<u>*Breaking Point*</u>

The mind can think but so hard before it wanders and wanders and tells itself to put up a guard. The eyes can only cry so many tears before it runs out of liquid or runs dry from the years. The ears can tolerate any sound until deception and time start to tear them down. The mouth can smile but wait a while and those teeth will disappear for a frown and scowl. The heart can tolerate so much before pain becomes an unbearable touch. The heart can only take so much unless love, true love is in its clutch.

Buckets of Understanding (My Misunderstandings)

Happiness escapes me, but I don't know why.
I don't relate well with most others because
they don't know my insides . . .

Stop & Go

Nothing to say. The mind draws a blank like an open field with no one there. Silent and slow. The distance between what I know and what I think widens and disappears without a blink.

That fast? I won't last.

Then right after that I return to my past. The rush hour traffic of thoughts in a flash. Too much to speak of, too complex a path. But why can't I focus?

Power Trip

How can I ever live without my title? It gives me power. It gives me hope. It allows me to separate what I have from what you don't.

Where would I be without the objects I own? Probably lost, like a king who is missing his queen, castle, and thrown. But in that case what do I do when those items are gone? Will I be devastated? Will I think my life is over?

If I am self-aware I won't because I'll know my role amidst all of life's temporary thrills. If not I'll learn the hard way to appreciate the reality of life's ills.

Equally Separate

Don't say it. We'll let the tension in the room speak for itself. I am the dark shadow in a world full of clouds. Whatever space I occupy most clouds will move around.

But I am not to be denied. Embrace my differences. Don't be afraid.

We are still alike though we operate in different ways. We both look better within the sun's rays or with the light of the moon to highlight our features.

So why alienate me to be different and "less" than you when the truth of it all is that you aren't really in control either?

[Subliminal Message]

I am an endangered species. Your research can't reach me. Data doesn't understand me so the textbook can't plan for me.
[Teachers can't teach me]

They hunt for me to put me in a cage then display me to others and teach them my ways. Even since it's been agreed to save rare breeds like me, my life remains a mystery.
[Teachers can't teach me]

It appears that I'm afraid but really I question how to behave. When I'm welcomed in, they place me under the microscope. I am alienated. There is no hope.
[Classes don't reach me]

I come to learn but am only taught about those that are just like me. So there's no surprise that this is not where I want to be!
[Schools won't meet me]

Ability

You say I either have it or I don't.

I say show me the way and I'll give you more than you could ever hope.

You say I'd waste your time if you had to sit and walk me through.

You'd rather complain of the things I can't do.

I say you're blind because I am far more than you can see.

A little patience would bring success for you and me.

Young and Black

Be a part of the future if you choose. Or be a part of the past and lose.

Some embrace you to show you the way. But you deny that love and instead go astray. Why do you behave this way?

Be a part of the future if you choose. Or be a part of the past and lose.

No respect for others. No respect for self. So you can't see your potential and won't appreciate any help. Blind to the blessings, that life has dealt.

Be a part of the future if you choose. Or be a part of the past and lose.

Hope is lost or so it seems. Life is larger than these trivial things. The only danger is that you might be too scared to pursue your dreams.

Be a part of the future if you choose. Or be a part of the past and lose.

Get it Right

Don't be confused. You want to know why they're afraid of you? I'll tell you why. It's not for the reasons you think. It has nothing to do with acting wild and talking loud. It has only to do with the fear of what you would be if you got it right.

If you did that, who you could be is someone that is out of sight; who they couldn't contend with-or defeat with all of their might. But instead you choose to be a child in flight. You think you're strong? They know damn well you've got it all wrong. You've been running all life-long. Only rather than stand and fight for the cause you've sold yourself short. At this rate your life will be cut short.

Your path says death, jail, drugs. You are correct that they shun all the above. But they don't fear that and they don't fear you. Because you've got it all wrong my friend. That is the truth.

<u>*PYT's*</u>

Pretty young ladies. My how I love to watch you from afar. Walk that sweet walk. You look so good. I don't remember how different we are until I hear you talk that young talk. It is then I realize the distance between us.

You say what you want right now. I know what I need for the long run. Those things don't add up. But I want you to know that I see the potential. If you only saw what I see, you'd be ok to wait patiently and present yourself like a queen-to-be.

You deserve a real man who will treat you the right way, but right now I don't think you'd notice if he came your way. Take your time young lady and one day someone will be glad to say. You're my queen! I'll be waiting for that day.

TKO—Trust, Know One

Another day
Another shattered dream
Another broken promise
That leaves me with my guard up
I should just attack to keep you back
Because every time I let you in-you knock me to the ropes again
So I bob and weave
Waiting for you to slip
When you make a mistake the body shot is what I'll take
To repay you for the trust you break
You aren't who you claimed to be
But you are just who I thought you were
This is why I trust no one on earth but the one I know . . .
Me!

Buckets of Perseverance

Where do I belong? Not here! I haven't found that place yet. But I will not stop until I get there.

<u>Chance</u>

We hardly ever understand it.

But have to appreciate the way life unfolds like we never planned it.

That's the proof that it is out of our hands.

Because we live but some die and that's a thing called chance.

When it's my chance, my time, I just hope I've blessed the world with enough so they can learn my mind and feel my heart.

Accident

Crashed into the wall
Glass has been shattered
Bodies bruised
Minds battered
The fear of contact now exists
Need repairs but can't be fixed
Cries of pain
Tears of hurt
Used precautions but that didn't work
Left in shock but moving on
No telling when the trauma will be gone

C. L. Lewis

Dirty Red . . . A Tribute

I want to go back
Back in time when everything was so simple
When I looked in your eyes and saw joy
When you carried a smile with deep dimples
Over time we grew up and learned that life is HARD
We would experience much pain, carry hurt and wear scars
Becoming adults separated us
As we aged we grew apart so far
Now you are gone and there is nothing left but the Love held in
my Heart
There is no way to change life or God's mighty plans
I just wish I could go back to the last time we slapped hands
"I got love for all my family"
The words you shared with me as I could barely recognize the
man you'd grown to be
Tainted by this world, any fool can see
I just wish that I could go back
Not just back to the last time I saw you and wanted to kick it
with you a while-telling myself the next time I see you we would
catch up on old times
I lost that chance when we lost you
But can I go back to the days when we had no cares?
When all I had to do was walk down the block and see you sitting
on the stairs
Let's go back across the street and play football all day
Never grow up to know that one day we shall pass away . . .
But the world keeps on moving
We cannot get in its way
But there will always be love in my heart for you
That is here to stay

On the Rise

Chained and shackled as a little boy I never thought that it was right that I would have to keep up with the other kids throughout my life.

I started out behind. The butt of every joke. Things were piling on so high that I thought I should have no hope.

Time and time again I would think that I was stuck—and I would cry and I would fall . . . Not wanting to get up.

But on the day I was picked up, I made the choice to always fight. And work so hard from day-to-day that everything would be alright.

So when you see me now I stand—tall . . . A man that can't be held back.

So while it may have seemed that the chains were to keep me on the ground, it turns out they actually helped keep me on the right track.

Trapped

Trapped at the bottom of a ditch. Nothing to do but look up to the sky and think life's a bitch. Then I wonder why? I see people up above me walking all around this ditch. They never bother to listen to my cries. Even those who look down at me and see the pain in my eyes. Everyone keeps passing me by, no one lends a hand.

All I want to do is to climb out of this ditch and get where I belong; find somewhere I can call home. But instead I feel so lost because I am on my own. Yet I am not alone. There are many others in this ditch with me. We are alike in many ways: we have been isolated, rejected, and given hell as a home to live out our days.

If we put our heads together, I am sure that we could create a plan to get to the top. But whenever one of us finds a way up the ditch, the rest of us just stop and begin to sit and watch. Instead of working as a group, everyone looks out for themselves as they sit off on their own. Some of us embrace our home. Others want to dig a way out for only themselves even if this means using everyone else's dead dry bones.

So I sit at the bottom of this ditch, thinking about how life will continue to be a bitch until I die. Then the pain becomes so unbearable that I just fall to the ground, bury my head and cry. I'm trapped . . .

<u>*Behind Bars*</u>

I'm confused
If you want to block me in you've found the right way
Lock me alone in a room with nothing to say
Not able to be free or dare to express the good, bad, & ugly that
makes me—me
That's what I call prison
With that said my heart goes out to all those locked in them
Maybe misunderstood
Maybe just missed the opportunities early in life to use their gifts
for good
But me, I understand
I feel the same because I know that not many really know this Cam
Or the things in my mind . . . my visions or my plans
If I can't do my thing I might as well be locked down with you,
Because in that case my life is over
DAMN!

C. L. Lewis

<u>It's Coming—A New Day</u>

There's a lot for me to deal with right now

I almost feel overwhelmed

But I know that this is my time to be built into a stronger man

I know I must experience all that this low point has to offer me—

Before I can be rewarded, I must appreciate my struggles

So I'll face whatever is thrown at me right now . . .

Then ask for more with a smile and "thank you"

This is the only way to let God guide me to my blessings

When my time finally comes

Inspirational Buckets

I need to be thankful. Most times I ask God why? He says down to me, "I've got plans for you. You will make a difference in this world even if you don't want to!"

Back to the Basket

Do I spin or do I fade?
With this person on my side that I must either overpower or evade
There's also others trying to stop me, but I don't fear defense
My team is strong so we can score at any minute

With the ball in my hand I turn and jump
My jump becomes a rise that no defender can touch
It's no longer my doing but still brilliant enough
I started back to the basket and ended with a slam dunk!

C. L. Lewis

<u>Questions</u>

How did I get here?
Where am I going?
What about progress? I feel like I'm slowing.
Who will I become?
I wish I was knowing.
When will my time come? As I keep going.
Why do I press forth? One day I'll show it . . .

<u>Reflection—Who Am I?</u>

An 'old-school' piece

Cool guy
Always on the move
Might very well make it big
Everywhere I choose
Ran away for a long while
Over and over again
Never thought I'd be a man absent from sin

Leave it to me
Evil I'd be'
Merely accepting mediocrity
Everyone else forewarning me
Let go of hurt and then you'll see
Love is in your heart and mind

Low and behold, they were right and I was blind
Each day is new
With a chance for me
In GOD I trust to
Set me free

Side-Track

After all the gifts that you've given to me, I get sidetracked with how others are living. The potential within is not enough for me. Nor the facts that I walk, talk, breathe, and see.

So disgraceful! How ungrateful? I get side-tracked with how others are living.

But the odd thing is with how others are living—is that they don't have the same tools I've been given. So I side-track them like they side-track me if they dare get caught up looking at me.

Instead of getting side-tracked with how others could be. I should cherish my own gifts, thankfully.

<u>*Regroup*</u>

My eyes are heavy and I just want to close them. Maybe keep them shut for a while is what I'm hoping. But I'm so tired that all I do is keep them open. And I stare so hard in front of me; you'd think that I'm focused. Today was such a hard day. I'm drained and feeling beat up. Even though there's still much more to do, I can only put my feet up. I'll regroup today so I can realize my way. The next stop is victory. I do see that-as clear as day.

A New Day

Shattered dreams when the sky goes from day to night . . . I am still here
Yet to reach the success of my destination
Uncertain, so I live in fear
Some nights I shake my head and question the outcome of my situation
But as time passes I know that the sun will again be here
To remind me of the hope of life and guide me toward my new beginning
I can see that the miracle is still unfolding
My story is incomplete—in fact it's yet to be told

So I'll outlast these difficult times for I am much tougher than any temporary circumstance could ever be. As each night comes to a close and the next day approaches I'll be thankful to the Most High for giving me another opportunity.

Legacy

Can't waste the time that I was given

I'm privileged so I need to celebrate my living

Every day to the fullest, handling my business

Then maybe help you to handle yours-that's the way I'm giving

But could I, would I, should I do more? I'd say I have to

Because that's what we're really living for . . .

And that's what we'll be remembered for after

Life & Loss

I took a Loss today . . . an emotional one.
But that's how life is. Maybe I am crazy. That's what I am.
Losing my mind with all that the world has to offer, and thus losing myself.

This is what growth is about. Taking falls—but standing back up tall.

Learning to love yourself and subsequently loving those around you.

Today I choose not to Lose myself in the mirror.
Today I will look outside, outdoors to the horizon and the beauty that is to come.

Check It

Could care less about money. I have no love for your cold hard green. To me it doesn't mean a thing. Except for the emotion it brings. Whatever that might be. It could be pleasant or it could be schisty. I spend it daily with disregard. Because I'll let my dues reflect my heart. I'll give and give for as long as I live. Knowing the Lord will see and hoping he'll forgive. My sins and mistakes and the ones I've yet to make. I'd rather sacrifice to give someone else a break.

Writer to Writer

Letter to TPS

You've sparked this mind. You are a hero because you speak your mind. I feel your heart. Your pain. Your dream. Your expression is genuine. One of a kind.

Your life was art and though physically gone I've learned a lot about myself through your rights and your wrongs. I've grown to be a man without you but I still know you're close by. You never quite left me and didn't say goodbye. But rather you've stayed back looking over my shoulder. To motivate me through all the tough times I see.

I feel that there is a part of you in me. But now it's on me-and me only. I've listened and learned. I'm grateful for what you've left me with. Now I'm ready to change the world.

Thank You

Lord I am not worthy but through it all you have stuck by me. Thank you

You have given me a wonderful family with whom I have shared struggles, laughter, joy, and pain. You have been my ROCK in my times of solitude—protecting me, watching me, loving me. You inspire me when I am down. You calm me when I am on the edge. You ground me so that I remain humble. You groom me through struggles. In all defeats you give me victory.
Thank You!

I am not worthy of your love and grace—most of us are not and yet you embrace us still. Thank You!

Your gifts are unparalleled so now I must spread the love that you have given us. Lord I am your servant and just as you have blessed me with the presence of others in my life to uplift me, I live to do the same.

Until the time that you call me home I will strive each day to represent you. Though I will often come up short you will be there to guide me through and finish the task.

When it is my time to join you, I pray that you will embrace my efforts and that what I do in life will be pleasing to you in the meantime.
Father . . . please show me the way!

<u>The Seed</u>

I am just a seed. The sun is looking down at me and it is my time to shine. I feel the mist of water from the sprinkler of knowledge as it approaches me. I extend my undeveloped shell as far as possible, trying to quench my thirst and grow.

I am patiently waiting to burst through the ground and share my inner plant with the world-adding beauty to the area that surrounds me and providing a fragrance that soothes the air. Whether I arrive to see grass, dirt, concrete, or even sand—I will leave an impression on this world that won't soon be forgotten.

I am just a seed. But soon I will become a mighty plant. Joining my brothers and sisters of life, producing my own little seeds that I can groom and watch grow. When the time comes that I should wilt or be cut down—my seeds, stump, and roots will remain as a symbol of this plant that was once just a seed.

Phase 2: Crunch Time

<u>*Goodbye*</u>

When its time to say goodbye give me a moment please. Allow me to share these last thoughts with the world I beg you. Lord I know you've been with me through so much. You've strengthened me through the bad times. Through my pains you've been my crutch. At times I know I've disappointed you so. At times I've wanted to run away I've disgraced you so much so. But as I'd approach the point of no return you'd always say "NO." And you'd call me back home. You've shown me signs to remind me that your love is stronger than any of my wrongs. So when its time to say goodbye I will gladly embrace the chance to say hi to you. But before I go I still need to share more with those who I may leave behind.

<u>To my family</u>: I love you all more than any words can share. Through all my tough times I knew each of you would always be there. I knew my laughs with you could erase even the worst of my tears. I know that our struggles together helped me to overcome many of my fears. Oh mother I love you because I am absent without you. I've always sought to be well-rounded based on the things I've seen you do. For me and the guys you'd sacrifice it all. For me and the guys you've been both mother and father, teaching us to stand tall. For my dad I wish it could have been different. But at the same time I'm grateful for what I've been given. I hope that at some point the words on this page won't carry the same meaning. We can fill in the blanks and strengthen what our team is. That means my brothers (your sons) who I wish I knew better. If I say goodbye now I'd say one day we'll be together. At that time we'll make up for the time that we lost. Then at some point with dad all our paths will be crossed.

To the brothers I've grown with I've left you in good faith when I go. I've given what I can and what I thought would help you grow. You'll be the young men that I know you can be. That will make me so proud. So just please remember me. Don't forget the love that mom passed down through me. That I have for you and I know you guys love me too. When I say goodbye, Benny you are next in line. Never forget the gifts you have inside. You can be anything that you are willing to try. I know that to be true so please keep that in your mind. Despite the trials of your journey, you will one day rise. So when that time comes I will not be surprised. To Micah, you've been such a joy to my life. A reminder of the miracles that God has in His sights. Continue to live your life to the fullest. And help others to appreciate the simple things we often forget. To 'lil Cam the newest addition, I love you nephew. I'm grateful to be mentioned as the person your named after. You've filled me with joy and laughter. I've seen my family grow through the weather. So as I say goodbye I ask that you continue to improve us and make the family names better. Both mine and your father's.

<u>*To my friends*</u>*: when its time to say goodbye I'll want you to know how much you've helped me. You've kept me sane and probably protected me. You've shown me how to love and care. And give me support when I've thought there was none there. I hope that through it all, I've been able to return. The love, honor, and blessings I've earned from you.*

<u>*To those that I don't understand and who have not been able to understand me*</u>*: I want to apologize for our misunderstandings. Whatever my doings have been toward you, know that they were not planned. Please forgive me as I have worked to forgive you in becoming a man.*

<u>*To those that struggle but persevere*</u>*: you've taught me so much. You must understand that it is my heart you have touched. I once heard*

that upon hard times we should not pray for those tough times to end. But rather pray that times reach their worst so that the real lessons can begin. With all that I've learned from you I feel like I win. Because the impact you've had on my life is that of a friend. So I say we are . . .

To the love I've known:
I say thank you. To my love I say I'm sorry. I've done you both good and bad. For that I do worry. As complicated as I've made things with you, I can't say I'd trade any of the things we've been through. When I say goodbye, my heart goes out to you. If goodbye is today there's still work left to do. So I'll think about the family that I always wanted but never had. I'll think about the lost highlight of being a father and dad. It hurts not having the chance to grow old with a large family. Most of all, I'll regret not sharing my life with a bride and wife. One who could ignite each one of my days, and soothe each of my nights. It hurts not to be a husband or experience forever. But I'm satisfied that you gave me at least a sample taste of your pleasure. So a goodbye to you is more than a phrase. It's a message that the mere thought of you has helped me to continue through some of my most hopeless days. I owe you much more than I could ever pay.

When it's time to say goodbye I want my message to be heard. When it's time to say goodbye I won't, instead I'll leave you with the memory of these words.

C. L. Lewis

Let Go—Let's Go!

I feel so gifted
Feel so lifted
I can finally realize the gift that you've given
The one that's for me
My talent, I see . . .
A something that I do so naturally
Not something I planned or something I understand
But the thing that I do, and the thing that I am
A voice to the people
An echo of you
The life that I live now
The things that you've shown me through
The hope for tomorrow
I'm finally ready
Empty buckets are temporary
The future is looking heavy
Let's go . . .

Summary

This poetry collection will seek to tell you a progressive story through each piece. In the Mr. Buckets phase of the book, I explore different elements of who I am. Mr. Buckets is a nickname that was given to me within the recent years by my close circle of friends, and thus in this section I tell a small portion of my individual story through poem.

The Buckets of Love phase follows, and this represents the primary storyline within the collection. Here, the poems I've provided explore the elements of romance from a unique perspective. First, during the 'Warm-up,' I share the inner-dreams of a person who is seeking a companion as well as the initial period of encounters between two love interests. Shortly after I transition into 'Crunch Time,' which explores the point in life where the novelty of romance has faded and the reality of breakup has occurred. Overall this phase of the book provides a snapshot of my own romantic experiences through verse.

As I move into Buckets of Understanding (My Misunderstandings), the purpose is to explore areas of life that I am working to better understand. Here I use my poetry both to express the stress of misunderstandings from my perspective, and also try to make amends for any confusion caused on my behalf.

Buckets of Perseverance is my salute to everyone who has experienced hard times in their life, and has either overcome those situations or is constantly putting forth their best effort to do so. In my own life circumstances I can relate. But I also understand that there are people who endure far more than I have or ever will, and to these people, I want you to know that you are on my mind and heart.

Finally, Inspirational Buckets are my offering to the Most High. Here my goal is to demonstrate my thanks and my understanding for why I am who I have become. It concludes with a period of "Awakening," where I communicate my realization for my life as I see it at the moment.

Concluding Remarks

When you read Empty Buckets I hope you feel like you've learned a bit about me. Moreover, I hope you find aspects of it that you can relate to in your life. But if neither of those are true, I would ask that you be open-minded enough to embrace my offering nevertheless; perhaps giving yourself a chance to be exposed to something (someone) different, or even reminded of such basic principles in life that you've known for some time. The creation of this collection has been my opportunity to grow.

I've also long wanted to express myself and be heard. Completing this piece has given me the chance to do both. I say "thank you" to everyone who has taken the time to let me share some of my life through these pages. Whether you've read the entire book or just one excerpt, it makes a great difference in my life that you would 'listen,' which is one of the most honoring things you could do for me. I pray that this book can make even the smallest of differences in your life in return. I am unsure where I go from here, but as far as the Lord will allow, I strive to move forward. Peace . . .

Index

Breinigsville, PA USA
13 July 2010
241661BV00001B/64/P